Wild Domestic

Wild Domestic

Poems

Natania Rosenfeld

The Sheep Meadow Press
Rhinebeck, NY

Designed and typeset by The Sheep Meadow Press

Distributed by The University Press of New England

Library of Congress Cataloging-in-Publication Data

Rosenfeld, Natania.
  [Poems. Selections]
  Wild domestic / by Natania Rosenfeld.
      pages ; cm
  ISBN 978-1-937679-44-6
  I. Title.
  PR6118.O85A6 2015
  821'.92--dc23

                        2014035640

All inquiries and permission requests should be addressed to the publisher:

The Sheep Meadow Press
PO Box 84
Rhinebeck, NY 12572

For Neil

CONTENTS

I. Mother Hunger

II. Prey

III. Wild Domestic

Wild Domestic

I.

Mother Hunger

The Ardabil Carpet

I saw effulgence:
a spoked comet,
its subject stars
prostrated.
The world made
anew, its yellow
monarch spinning
in viridian stillness.

"Unknown" whether
this lustre lay on
sanctuary or palace
floor. For prayer
or pleasure, all
are beckoned.

Mother Hunger

When you came down, summer
afternoons, from the attic,
with baskets for the two of us,

shadows hung in the porch.
I followed your stained fingers,
scratched ankles between rows

of berries. You stood, flicked
away the strands sticking
to your eyelids, looked out

somewhere I couldn't see.
You filled your basket fast.
In July, we climbed ladders,

silent among cicadas,
and chose the plumpest cherries.
Our Dodge racketed past

collapsing barns and shacks,
bearing a sweet smell. At night,
fruit waited unwashed,

drowning in its juice,
calling in your dream like
the pines near Klaipeda, or

the hiss of red ashes
in stubble fields

where you and your sister wove
a fruit tapestry,
impaling apples

on charred stalks. Next day,
when you gorged on fruit,
I lost you again.

All She Remembered

(Bertha Rosenfeld, 1904-1991)

Look, this is all I can tell you:
I was sick the whole time
on the boat, I didn't know where
I was going. My father was
a man in a picture: first, with a beard,
then, later, without. His face didn't
tell me anything about him, or about
my new mother and two strange sisters.
I was seventeen. I made two friends
on the way, but we parted, and I never
heard from them. I think one went
to Wyoming—imagine, Wyoming!
Some people kept kosher on the ship
and arrived skin and bone; I never
cared enough to sacrifice my health.
To be honest, my belief is not deep.
I know if we honor His commandments,
God is supposed to care for us, but
I always believed what I could see.

The first night on Ellis Island, I dreamt
of my mother. You know that she died
giving birth to me. I never saw her,
or heard her voice singing. That night
she came to me. She wore a long white
dress and her red hair shone down
to her waist, the way young women
wore their hair, until they married
and had to shave it off or cover it. She said
to me—in Yiddish, of course—*Tokhter,*

it will be all right. So I believed her.
What choice did I have? Either it
would be all right, or it wouldn't. Better to
believe it would. May she rest in peace.

The Statue of Liberty, I don't remember.
I know my friends tried to make me look
when we were coming into port, but I could
only worry about what lay ahead. I'd traveled
across Russia, it was a bad time, a dangerous time,
a girl by herself, to the port in Riga—
and I wasn't afraid! But all I remember
from my arrival is fear.

Autobiography

A child, I entered German
churches, pitied the gaunt man
hanging from open hands
like my father's. I drew
his picture, brought it to him
at morning.

They told me our God
had no face.

I must learn
and immerse myself
to be a Jew.

•

A cold, white lightbulb
lit the *mikveh*: lonely
like all Jewish places.
The silent *rebbetzin*
covered my head
with a washcloth,
and the rabbi listened
behind a door half-open
to a naked girl's chant.

That chill summer day
belied me.
When was I not a Jew?

On my stern father's lap,
I learned from books.
My mother's face still
knew panic: she'd watched
madmen waving crammed
trains from stations,
the faces pressed against slits.

•

Whom did I bless
in the narrow bath?
Our words ascend
to an averted keeper,
the red sun flares
in a loosened fist.

Mother without name
or country, father who speaks
unhating,
the murderer's tongue—

you gave me songs
in a stained language:

Herr, es ist Zeit . . .
Du bist wie eine Blume . . .

To you I give back
my sticklegged words.

Stuttgart, 1969

Foolish to imagine
you were ever unafraid.
There I am, face sticky
with ice cream, my father's fingers
ready to blot the stain
with his saliva.

Each morning I was sick
before climbing
the endless steps
to the *Waldorfschule* on the hill.
Others mocked me:
they owned leather satchels,
I did not. Across
the street from us,
Schottstrasse Sieben,
lived a blond, neat boy
with a scooter. He whizzed
down the hill and walked
manfully back up.
Evenings, I stood
in my pyjamas watching him.

The sky there
was blue as an eye.
Behind our house,
you could look into the valley
city, green and brown, snug
like a scene on a cuckoo clock.

Friday nights, my father
took me to the rebuilt synagogue.
The rabbi reached down,
stroked my hair. I drank
from the red cup,
then returned to my place
beside my father, among
the widowers.

1945

Opa tied beneath the wagon as you
passed the guards, and Oma showed
the papers. Always, papers.
Then, the little town—the inn,
where you lived way up, under
the roofbeams, with sheets for walls.
Hopping down four flights to
the bakery, its kitchen basement,
powdered with flour, you carried
his cigarette: a work of butts
that you'd collected and he'd
combined into one stick you lit
from the oven. Poking a finger
in the yellow, rising dough like
a baby's belly, pinching a raisin,
swiping a bit of sticky icing, before
you puffed (*You've got to keep it
lit, Stassi!*) your way back up. Beneath
the roof, he waited like a tired king
(I loved him, too, when I was
your age), took it from your little
hand, inhaled the American scent
in his still-strong, still-heaving lungs.

Levelings

My aunt
was a steeple.
Sadness fell
from her peaked nose.
Her eyes were pointed
tiles. Her mouth
was a holy window.
I looked up and up,
listening. The word
was lovely girls stricken
in the doorway
of adolescence. I must
consider very carefully,
gravely, my strong
desire to abjure
the flesh of animals.
Vegetables are not enough.
I must think
of my dear parents,
my "homeless" mother,
oceans away, my dark father,
hunched
in Hebraic study.

Oh aunt, I thought,
female of angles
and flutey forbiddings.
Go away. Be my friend.
Oh odious . . . The sun
shone through pea-green
trees, the grass was

furrowed like lettuce,
hazelnuts beckoned everywhere.

Now all beings
are smaller; buildings, too.
The day I went home,
I ate a sausage
(but never told).
I know some secrets:
your illness, your flaws,
your hot tears
in the afternoon. Please,
dear, take good care: eat,
drink, jubilate. This
level, domeless place
still is lush.

Little Fly

(Louise Bourgeois, James Joyce)

Two gnarled legs in her fists,
the other six sprawled across

the wall as if the monster'd
tried to flee. *The spider is my*

mother, she grins. Kiddo,
grip Ma's limbs! She drags

you up, you pull her down.
Beneath her belly, lack

becomes plenty. The sticky
threads will tangle; persevere,

don't thrash, wrap them round
your arms like phylacteries.

One day you'll fly by those nets.

Such Hungers

A woman was dying
in travail. Her sickness
wrapped her in fog, but once
she had a visitation of blue grapes.

She reached for them,
and they were gone,
leaving her tongue acrid
and flicking with desire.

II.

Prey

Four Rabbits by Soutine

I.

He hangs in blue ice,
a dead branch.
His waist pinched
like a greyhound's,
hind feet like a child's
in oversized socks.
The front paws flail
before the nose,
blood crusts his eyes.
Plucked from the cradle,
hurled at the wall.

II.

Hare with Forks is crucified,
decaying on a pond-scum
green cloth. The forks,
crude paws, are
ready to tear. The rabbi,
ninety, was flayed
"with iron combs."
In childhood, his brothers
beat him green and black.

III.

This one's not for sale.
Odette awaiting Swann
has feasted, been feasted
upon. Her repose dares
you to tear her flesh.
You wouldn't do it:
the fur's like
pussy willow. If she
has a soul, it hops
in fields where foxes
enter on their bellies.

IV.

Flayed Rabbit: anatomized,
used up, on the stained
sheet. The torso stretched
like pulled meat,
a skull, vacant bloody
mouth at the point
of the genitals.
Thrown down, or laid
gently, the thin arms
still rise in a screech
beside the head.

Look for truth:
you'll find gristle.

Soutine, *Two Pheasants on a Table*

"Sing!" said the butcher,
and they sang, in falsetto voices,
in squealing soprano. "Dance!"
he commanded, and they
pirouetted with buckling
ankles. "Now lie down."
The necks were quickly
cracked. Blood filled beaks,
feet were stained, they lay
like two dirty handkerchiefs.

Fantasia

Just once, some days, I'd like
to stop being a Jew. My heart,
that slumping ancient, would sit
upright, clean edged, like
an earnest student with jug ears.
History would be a nodding matter.
Oh yes, says the pointer, *this*
and this. —Charlemagne the same
to me as any other bloody man.
Cleansed, those figures would
process across the map—clean,
in white robes, with goatees.
No mess, not this lament, not
this racking laughter. No pecking
with my perpetual beak, none of this
But what and *But suppose.* A serene
letting-say what they may say, and
at night, on the pillow, a head
like water. In dreams, no beckoners,
no red-on-black, but a piping
of sopranos in radiant skirts. And
at morning: the hunchback business
over, no gaberdine, no turning
on the news, no girding and no asking.
A vast clarity, like a tent.

Bodies

When he lies on his side with his back to me, my man's buttocks
are round like a woman's and white as an eggshell. On his hip,
a palm-sized spot cool and smooth as a flat stone lifted from
the streambed. His wisdom: dark and temperate. My heart, the
organ I say I love him with, is not much different from the sirloin
the gangster relishes after a night's work.

At night, he sleeps peacefully. I awaken on our red flannel
sheets, nearly black in the streetlamp's half light. His body is like
a splash of milk. I reach for the wise spot on his hip. Unlike
our friend's lover, diabetic double amputee, he has both legs. I
have both legs. I have a scar in the middle of my body, but the
doctors healed me. They laughed in the hospital room and drew
diagrams. I am afraid, but lucky.

I love to nibble at him: shoulder, ear, neck, buttocks. A pillow for
my sad face, my head full with bodies.

*

In the hospital they said, "Your belly was full of brown syrup.
We rinsed you out." Youngest woman on the cancer ward, I
didn't have cancer. Mother hovered in her red sweater, the color
of ketchup (my blood is chocolate-colored, so the explorers
of my gut taught me)—the first thing I saw, coming out of
anesthesia.

*

Elizabeth I, the Faerie Queene, receiving delegations, displayed
her breasts. The French ambasssador's account describes her
with bodice open to the navel. "Prince," she called herself. And
she wore a headdress like a vulva. On love notes, a heart with the
shape of a vulva. Twin wings, a butterfly.

In the execution movie, the man's put in a diaper before he goes to the chair. Slaughterhouse workers wade through shit and blood. I won't eat mammals, but I devour seafood for the flesh consistency.

Awake at night, unbreathing, I grasp for what the rapist and killer said to his victims. If I can get through the "dialogue," I'll be safe. I know it from stories I've heard. He wants her to tell him she likes it.

I read about the torture *bastinado*: beating and flaying of the soles of the feet. I read about Armenian women dancing as they're whipped, gasoline poured on them, then lit. "Dance, bitches!" In the shtetl called Konin, writes Theo Richmond, Jewish women were forced to dance around burning Torah scrolls.

Song

He stretched
　　　his muzzle
at the sky, black against
　　　night his eye
glinted over me,
　　　the muscled
withers a lava sea.
　　　I reached
upward, his mane
　　　burned me, the
eye sparked, *I'll*
　　　break you, I said,
but he'd tamed me.

Danger in My Garden

White hawk
rose, flapped down.

I ran to the fence,
watched him haul

himself way up
I saw at my feet

a rabbit sprawled,
belly open. By the legs

I lifted, dropped
it in the garbage.

Deep down in
the bin, the chestnut

eyes still stare in fear..

Assyrian Relief

Is it not enough to have shot an arrow
straight into the lion's brow?

As the beast embraces him, the king
drives a sword through his chest.

The front paws are splayed, each
claw stretched in mortal despair.

Must he also smile, his little attendant,
bearing the quiver, smirking along

while the great cat, so finely furred
and muscled, every millimeter

chiseled with artisan's love, draws
back his lip and howls, howls, howls?

Stranger

Encaged,
feet steeped,
head bowed,
beak grazing
water's surface,
I stood hours and days.

Every so often
they fed me
something hard,
pushing it in
to the slit of my mouth.

I swallowed
without lifting or
turning my head,
without shifting
body or feet.

When they came
to check on me
the water I stood in
was thick red.

Just a bird, they said,
a hawk from
somewhere else.
We didn't put her there.

In Warsaw

A forest of graves
in a far corner of the city,
far from the *Assembly Place*.

Snails, gray, dun, spotted,
rest on inscriptions, slide
in their grooves. Spiders on
the slanted stones, the path
to the gate. Almost touching
grass, branches bend down.

In the air, the unburied.

Historical Observation

In the hotel tower
we slept deeply

our white sheets
changed daily if

we wished, single
malt and world news

at the touch
of a finger, plush

towels, a view, where
the ghetto burned.

Earthward

Hair white, indigo-eyed,
Mother calls me to the last
flaring of her summer garden.

On our evening walk, Father's
head turns slowly when I point
to the still egret by the pond.

Midnight, cicadas' frettings
mark my sleep. At dawn, brittle
shells litter the lawns. I bend

to look at thin, veined wings.
"Bury me," my father says,
"without ado in a pine coffin."

"Do what you like," says
my mother, "with my ashes."
In their living room, I hold

each one's hand. Beebalm
flames beneath the window.

Admonitions

I saw a shining, dark blue bird on the grass, unable to move. I bent and saw its neck was choked in a band, the head turned wrong way around. I put my hands around the bird and was able to pick her up and unwrap the noose. Instantly, her head turned around the right way and grew normal-sized, and she flew free.

*

"How can we atone?" they chanted. "Revive all the birds you murdered," I said. They took slingshots, held them up, tried to coax the stones back in, but the stones lay mute and unmoving yards away on the barren ground. "You see," they said, "there's nothing to be done." "Then," I said, "I will take away your book of birds." And I took it, and wound it in wire so that it could never again be opened. If they needed to identify the remaining bird species, they would have to find a new language.

*

They say the god entered her in the form of a bird. I say change the old stories to new ones. Say that he was the sky and she was the bird and he cradled and carried her. Say that he was the pond and she was the stork and drank from him. Say that he was the tree and she pecked at his bark and was fed deeply. Even say that she lost herself in the maze of his twigs. Only don't say that he entered her in the form of a bird. If I could dictate the laws, I would make it against the law to say that.

Omen in Cornwall

On the cliffside
we looked down:
uncountable gulls
roosted there in pairs.

At our voices
they hurtled up,
around and above us,
blotting the sunset
like a white sheet.

Not a beak opened.
We heard only
flapping, no cry.
We stood without
breathing.

Then air and sea
were dark, the crag
was clotted with ghosts.
Nothing left
but to go back home.

Idyll at Drigg

"Return for tea," they said.
We ran to the dunes, their
thick blond grass pushing
upward, against the wind.
Sheep lifted vague faces, resumed
gazing at the gray flank
of sleeping sea. Above us,
a lark sailed, swooped, twittered.
You tumbled down these ridges
as a child, played made-up games,
burned your sore calves in surf.

Now a child stands below us
with his red pail, wavering,
in the shadow of the nuclear
plant. Which way to run?
Seawrack and garbage,
beached jellyfish veined green,
the curling waste of tunneling worms
surround him. "Come," you say,
"return for tea." We dry our feet,
kiss, and climb from poison
through the fierce, firm grass.

Encaustic

—for Ellen Trumbo

Against my starched hospital sheets, Fayum faces
gaze forth, thick-lashed, defiant, skins gleaming

chestnut, curls slick olives. I press the morphine
button and dream: Demetrios, who's paid

the boatman, calls my name. Alexis, upper lip
fuzz-bright, offers kisses. One grandmother,

leathered by years of desert sun, takes my wrist
and flicks the needle out. I start awake, tremble,

and check my pallid face in the mirror the nurse
brought when I had to see myself: gaunt; still here.

For Omm Sety

I.

"Bentreshy, your bad little heart calls to my heart,
and my sad old heart runs to you . . ."

At fourteen I found
my master's dead face
in a marble house.
At thirty I went to Abydos
to find him.
There I married one
with soft, carved Pharaoh lips,
and waited.

The floating loon
swoops in the river for fish.
Like any visitor
in his best white galabiya,
he came at last,
crossed the threshold
from the balcony.
His fingers were dry
as papyrus.
He touched my heavy breasts,
locked his thumbs in mine.

II.

"He stayed with me all night, and made love
to me in a surpassing way."

His lips, calfskin velvet
pressed my ear, and the leaves
of Memory fell open.

At the lily pool
he saw me first:
the small priestess
with hair like wheat
and blue lotus eyes.
He called to me.
When I sat by him,
he trembled like reeds
in river wind.
Little one, he said,
they will find you out
and leave me
with my sad, old heart.
It is all destined.

I became his Nūt,
night tent, light of dawn.
The moon rode my back
and I bore the red sun
between my thighs.

III.

*"I said, 'You are not old, my Beloved, and you
will not be lonely any more tonight. Come.'"*

It was only this
I waited for, dancing in a houri's dress
in my father Reuben Eady's
Palladium Cinema at Plymouth.
For every misstep, he beat me,
little tailor turned impresario.

His tiny eyes saw nothing.
My mother, when she found
my nightdress torn
from neck to hem in a line
like the trickle of blood
down a bride's thigh, shook
at my possession. But in Abydos,
one night, she saw Him come to me
with a robe over his galabiya
blue as the river depths.

Country of dust and graves,
they scorned you. Master who
lay by me years of nights,
I alone knew you. Your tired face
rests in my palm, you hold
my other hand; we are not old,
we have found our final home.

III.

Wild Domestic

Fish Songs

The old ones tell stories
of the great carp in the family tub.
Skin flecked by scales, the children
itched for escape.

See them now, vociferating
in large houses!
Even in this age, they wave
their fins about, wobble
on nervous tails, rock
like frightened guppies.

•

Fish think. In this picture,
observe the pensive trout,
gazing at a pine above the dark
stream. Branches bend, needles
approach scales, silent song rises.
Oh! Cries the fish, for that is all
a fish can utter. *Oh* like
the heart's hole, *oh* through
which water flows, *oh* like a pond.

At the Zoo

The rhinoceri were cantering
I swear it,
round their mud pond.
Their step was gay
and grave. I stood
far away, at the wall, not even a mote
in the eye
of a rhinoceros.

Oh mud hide. They say
your tusk is only hair,
though built to frighten.
I would like to touch it
and learn your way
to gravely canter
'round the pond

then lie down
with my mate,
snuffling the dust,
unconcerned
by flies, and perhaps
a small gray bird
perched on my unfeeling
rump, chattering
its little song.

Snail's Pursuit

I.

"Peace," says the soprano,
retired to the sea, "is this tide
licking the stilts of my house."
Her toe strokes the rug,
she flicks an ash, goes early
to bed with a glass of gin.

In her closet, a red cloak
keeps Aida's sweat from 1963.
Mornings, she strolls the winter
beach, white hair touching
scarlet shoulders. *O terra, addio.*

II.

The Chinese masseuse leans
her palms on a sill above
Main Street, hears the howl
of the Burlington Northern
Santa Fe. Grandmother bent
to pick rice in Yunan Province.
What are these empty streets,
fields of alien corn?

She starts the tape of reed
flute melodies, attends the next
body's tide, same West
or East, home or away, thin
or fat with strange food.
Always currents to listen to.

III.

The girl kept goldfish in a bowl,
a snail to clean their leavings.
When the bright fish died,
she watched him climb the glass,
feelers quaking. He pursued
the algae, blazing a trail, his
toothed tongue scraping.

The panes turned opaque.
Sometimes a ray pierced his
mossy domain. Did he feel
her presence when she tapped?

Annunciations

for LL

I see a spiral foot,
an eye with ten
long lashes, wings.
I see a small person
on a surfboard with
a yellow platter behind
his head. I see a girl
reading a novel in
a blue dress, wondering
what happens next.
An androgyne
clearing his throat.
Vein in the girl's
forehead, a small bruise
at her neck. Interruption,
truncation. Light in the sky,
throbbing, insistent.
I feel the end coming.

You see purple,
a floor of polished marble
slanting down
as if to touch you
on the chest.
You see a hand
upraised, luminescent.
Unafraid, you take
brush in hand,
dip and leap.

Hammershoi

(Danish painter, 1864–1913)

I.

In the room filled with gelid
light, white, frigid sky
in the panes, a servant stands

before an empty table, ample-
hipped, back a dark expanse,
gazing at something in her

hands, and trembles with rage.

II.

He's stared at the nape
of his wife's neck for so long
he's fixed an arrow there.

She stands looking out, between
iron-framed twin beds.
The sill is stainless, jug empty,

beyond the single branch a cloud
waits to let go its burden of
early snow, and she wonders,

Can I still turn back?

Calatrava

A bird is a bone is
a back is a bridge.
The spine bending
is the wing curving,
its white tip
brushing eternity.

A house is a stair
is a ladder is a neck.
Like lover's vertebrae,
the boxes rise to the sky.
The happy believer
broods in his aerie,
a block of four stories
above others the same
and others the same

with only God to speak to
or, in God's absence,
a stray swallow.

High in the Air

We two play all the figures
spinning
like horses
impaled on poles.

One day a hunchback,
yesterday
the Fat Lady,
today I'm narrow as a pin.

My yellow-armed
trainer drove West.
He appears
in a lowslung town
where the sun
is mottled like salami.

He followed the blonde—
as we all do:
for she is like bait
(though laced
with ground glass).
She swings from the tent roof
with dreams of her own.

•

I grew
a moustache yesterday,
a demure
fringe of stiff black hairs.
I could have

charged admission:
Mouth like an Eye!
Mouth like a Cunt!—

but the affliction passed.

Who are we? Sparrows scold the huge
cat;
she sits licking in her cage.
Cold spouse, clenched like a pea:
I turn to whip you and I see
the slender line down your torso,
blood beading from it
like pomegranate seeds, the tiny
thrumming at the edges
of the beautiful slit
you made for me.

Walking Harakiri Man.

•

The acrobats will convene,
like it or not,
sometimes in tulle,
sometimes in tennis shoes,

unionizing
in flutey voices.

It's they who control us.

A dark pine
sees its own reflection,
leans into the pond,
needles sweeping fluid.

Come, take my hand,
illumine my changes.

Bandits

Souls in mouths,
wood beneath chins,
we make sparks
and dance by them.

My little girl offers
a flower, first purple
clover of the year, petals
tender as a lower lip.

She'll wither by day's end.
La la, we shout, *I'm
lonely, I'm drunk, I've
beaten my woman again.*

We whistle and stomp.
*Lie in my arms, I'll cook
meat you'll never forget,
a stew you can drown in.*

Soldiers, police, undertaker
with long hands: come.
You won't cut my blackbird's
wings, you can't bury the wind-

shaken grass. Come
night, greatest thief.

Her

She stamps, she bites,
she bares her chest—
she'll be broken
in the end, like the ebony
horse the groom leads
from the wings. But
for now, how she kicks
at her stall! Her feet
are bare, but this one
can walk on stones,
the sharpest—on knives,
if her love demands it.
See her in a fit, making
a storm of her skirts,
hoisting the soiled, scarlet
flounces so high above
the knee, you see muscle
like a man's. In her teeth
now a rose, now a dagger,
she slashes her world.

What I Want for My Birthday

A hankie like a quilt,
made from silks in every color,
with shimmering seams
and a snake's tongue of red.
A holiday under palms
where bronze men attend with balms.
One season in someone else's mouth,
a bed of plush for my impatient heart,
bangles for half-fat, half-muscled arms.
Love for pallid skin, and hairs
in the wrong place—tributes, even, to my beauty!
At last, a pet tortoise in a cage so large
she takes a day to get from end to end.
I will crouch down and look in her rough face,
and she will push her head straight at me
and give me wisdom from leathery eyes.
In the wee hours, I'll find her in her shell
and remember Beckett's Winnie, half-buried in earth.
Winnie, I'll call her, and trundle on another year.

Pastoral

You gave me a necklace:
silver links.
You said "Stray.
Stray if you like."

I went to the fence
and gazed. There
were only sheep, blurred
white forms, ruminative,
exposed. I know of wolves
in the hills. But even
a housedog can sink
her teeth in the taut,
pink neck of lamb.
Howls echo
in the pasture: the ewe
hears them and buckles.

Here is your face, succinct
and sharp. Your closed lids
like small purple leaves,
your soft, fluttering
neck-vein. The key
in your loosened hand.

All night I watch
and awaken late,
wordless and alone.
So begins my longing
and has no end.

Gift

Years long, we dug
to reveal it. Now
we will never stray

farther than a room,
keeping it in view,
swathed in the daylight

of our gaze, draped
with music like the green
sheet on twigs, like ginkgo

with its very early harps,
or like a root vegetable
that won't shake off

its birth-dirt, even
in the stomach. Because
of our labor, it must have

perpetual rest, free of
the bonds that tie even
squirrels, even birds, hardly

allowed to dive down
from their little branches.
It will lie lucent and unopened,

fallow in the core of our estate.
And the healer who led and
pointed, who watched us with

our raw hands, our stained rake
and spade, hoping us on,
shall have a house and figtree,

and his full view of woods and fields.

Behind Skiddaw

the brooding fell, we lay interlaced
in our summer bed. How does the cow

feel, udders aburst, teats like filled
thumbs of rubber gloves? From our window

we saw the calf buckle, mother bellowing,
shoving with her head, licking it all over with

her towely tongue. Oh, her ache! You left
before sundown. After lone supper, I walked out,

startled a brown-black heifer with yellow-
tagged ears. She flung her head, cantered

ahead of me in fear, parted her jaws and howled
till her fellows nosed the fence. Who was her farmer,

where her gate? Hands hanging, I stood
without clue. That night, among the sheep

ghosts, the baby we'd had and forgotten
lay in my arms. I offered my breast, she

guzzled and curled, white as cat or slug.
I laid her in a drawer and left.

Under the Plank

Unintended, im-
    mediately wanted.
Named for a singer
    with a dove's voice.
Home—bedded and
    beloved. Spoken to.
And more speaking,
    back and forth,
over my head
    and into it. Tongues,
dimly understood,
    then digested. Twirling
on the purple carpet
    to Tschaikovsky.
An assault—at nine—
    on *Crime and Punishment*.
The unkindness
    of others. Grappling
beneath my father's desk—
    a plank across two shelves.
My mother sad,
    absent—reading crime
novels on the sofa.
    Sex, like a chariot
and four. The hand
    at night releasing sparks.
Cruel boys. Errors.
    Suddenly, the sixth
decade. Still here,
    twirling.

Now, Father

Always, you said
"Stand up straight."

Upright in every sense,
you also counseled *neatness*

and *discipline*. Now your desk's
a harbor where the boats

have collided, masts akimbo,
sails in the water, the pilots

hiding, or drowned. And
your head emerges from

your shoulders like a turtle's.
Your hooded eyes shine with

Weltschmerz and amusement.

My Abductor

awaits, stamping, eyes agleam.
I'll grip his mane. Fused,

we'll bolt: vaulting the fence,
stunning frogs, crushing grass.

Moon-faced heifers, hay snufflers,
look up, gape! We're on fire,

woman and horse. We arc over
roofs, barnyard growing

small as a flea. Bellowing,
we call it out, with hooves

on air and feet on hide,
we tattoo our blood song

on the currents that bear us
far, so far from here.

Family Weather

Sometimes father approves.
Sometimes mother cries.

Either way, the clouds
float toward the horizon.

Birds, too, are dependable,
if you lie on your back

and watch closely. They lift
from the tree in swaths,

calling out. So, years later,
when the beloved leaves

your afternoon bed, you hear
singing and see snowbanks

and are never alone.

NOTES

"Mother Hunger": Klaipeda is a port city in Lithuania; before WWII, an international city with a large German presence. The German name of Klaipeda is Memel.

"Autobiography": "mikveh": ritual bath; "rebbetzin": the rabbi's wife. "Herr, es ist Zeit": "Lord, it is time," the opening of Rilke's "Herbsttag." "Du bist wie eine Blume": "You are like a flower," poem by the German-Jewish poet Heinrich Heine.

"For Omm Sety": Omm Sety, or "Mother of Sety" was an Englishwoman by the name of Dorothy Eady who, after a fall on the head as a child, responded with passionate recognition to the mummy of the Pharoah Sety I in the British Museum. As an adult, she moved to Egypt, and became the helper of a number of archeologists, uncannily able to guide them to sites of lost objects based on her own memory of her past life as a pharoah's mistress.

Nūt is the goddess of the sky.

"Encaustic": Encaustic, a painting style that involves wax, literally means "burned in." The Fayum Portraits are naturalistic paintings commissioned in late antiquity by wealthy Greco-Roman patrons in Egypt to cover the mummified faces of their loved ones.

"Calatrava": Spanish architect, born 1951.

"Behind Skiddaw": Skiddaw is a fell, or mountain, in the English Lake District.

ACKNOWLEDGMENTS

Thanks to:

Stanley Moss, extraordinary editor.

The Virginia Center for the Creative Arts, Ragdale, and the Jentel Foundation. Dean Larry Breitborde and the John and Elaine Fellowes Fund of Knox College for subsidizing travel and stipends.

More friends and loved ones than can be named, but some must be: Stella P. and Sidney Rosenfeld. Audrey Petty, Anna Leahy, Kitty Bancroft, Joan Landis, encouragers and interlocutors in Chicago and Philadelphia; Gabriel Levin, Simon Lichman and Zali Gourevitch in Jerusalem and Tel Aviv. Also in Philadelphia: Dave Bonanno, Arthur Vogelsang, and Mike Duffy. Elsewhere: Peter Balakian, an early mentor. Peter Covino, Joan Houlihan. Wayne Koestenbaum. And Lynette Lombard, for endless inspiration and celebration.

Thanks to these journals/anthologies for first publishing versions of these poems:

The American Poetry Review: "Flying High"
Another Chicago Magazine: "Bodies" (winner of an Illinois Arts Council Literary Award, 2007)
Calyx: "Little Fly
Cimarron Review: "Under the Plank," and "Soutine, Two Pheasants on a Table"
Exquisite Corpse: "Such Hungers," "For Omm Sety," and "At the Zoo"
Gettysburg Review: "Snail's Pursuit," "Calatrava," and "Family Weather"
Isthmus: "Earthward" and "What I Want for My Birthday"
Nimrod International: "Fish Songs," "1945," and "Idyll at Drigg"
POOL: "Annunciations"
Prairie Schooner: "Prelude"
Raritan: "In Warsaw" and "Assyrian Relief"
Saranac Review: "My Abductor"
The Best of Kore Press 2012: "In Warsaw"
Roger: "Omen in Cornwall"
Seneca Review: "Fantasia," "Admonitions," and "Autobiography"
The Waiting Room Reader (Cavan Kerry Press, 2012): "The Ardabil Carpet."